Images of DEVON

The front cover shows harvesting near Brampford Speke.
The back cover shows the harbour, Clovelly.
Inset pictures at each chapter opening are:
Half title page : Horse Bridge, Sydenham Damerel.
Title Page: the view from Bolt Head to Salcombe.
Frontispiece: the Bishop's Palace with the twin towers of the
Cathedral in the background.
The Coast: shipwreck at Hartland.
Towns and Villages: cottage at Buckland.
Rural Devon: Glen Lyn Gorge, Watersmeet.
Living in Devon: Traditional tar barrel rolling at Ottery St Mary,
held in November each year. Barrels of flaming tar are
carried on the backs of local men through crowded streets.
Dartmoor: Burrator in Winter.

Images of DEVON

Peter Thomas

WESTCOUNTRY BOOKS

First published in Great Britain by Westcountry Books, 1995

British Library Cataloguing in Publication Data
A Catalogue Record for this book is available
from the British Library.

ISBN 1 898386 17 X (paperback)
1 898386 16 1 (hardback)

WESTCOUNTRY BOOKS
Halsgrove House
Lower Moor Way
Tiverton
Devon
Devon EX16 6SS

Tel: 01884 243242
Fax: 01884 243325

Images of Devon is one of a series of books intended to capture the
essential and distinct character of the westcountry.

IMAGES TITLES IN PRINT:
Images of Exmoor

CURRENTLY IN PRODUCTION:
Images of Dartmoor
Images of Dorset

TO FOLLOW :
Images of Cornwall
Images of Somerset

Designed for Westcountry Books by Topics Visual Information.
Reprography by Peninsular Repro Services Ltd, Exeter.
Printed and bound in Singapore by SNP Printing Pte Ltd.

CONTENTS

FOREWORD

by
THE RIGHT REVEREND HEWLETT THOMPSON
BISHOP OF EXETER

This is a book with a message, but with very few words. The message is that Devon is
very beautiful indeed. Oh yes, there are days when it rains from morning till night
and the damp clouds sit just above our heads: they are the modest price of the
stunning beauty revealed in the photographs. As an ardent walker in many parts of
the county I treasure these pictures. They remind me of the many happy days and
hours spent out and about in this favoured part of God's creation.
They will be enjoyed equally by those whose good fortune is to
live here, and those who travel here on holiday.

+ Hewlett Exon:

THE PALACE
EXETER, DEVON

INTRODUCTION

Peter Thomas is fast becoming known as one of the westcountry's finest and most prolific landscape photographers and, being born and bred in Devon, his love for the county is reflected in every picture he takes.

In compiling a book of photographs about a particular place, it is tempting to select only the well-known locations with which everyone will identify. In choosing the pictures used in *Images of Devon* care has been taken to ensure that such favourite scenes are well-represented but that the more secret places of the county are included too.

The intention has been to produce a book for those who live in Devon, for visitors to the county, and those who have moved away and wish to be reminded of their county. The images here are chosen to remind them of home: the variety of the landscape, the unmistakable character of the towns and villages, and the breathtaking sweep of the high clifftops above a summer sea.

In producing such a book it is hoped that all those who walk Devon's byways, those who live in the county or have family ties there, or those who may have paid only the briefest of visits, will share equally in the enjoyment of these images of her glorious landscape.

AUTHOR'S PREFACE

Considering the importance, and beauty, of Devon it is surprising how little photographic coverage the county has received, other than for tourist purposes. In creating this book I have had in mind the need to fill this gap and to provide a portrait of the county which captures the essence of its people and landscapes and which will be enjoyed by resident and visitor alike.

As a Devonian and a photographer I appreciate the awesome nature of this task. Devon is the third largest shire county in Britain with a great variety of landscapes, from the soaring cliffs of North Devon, the bleak moorlands of Exmoor and Dartmoor, to the rolling acres of South Devon. In driving through the county it seems that every turn in its winding lanes uncovers yet another view worthy of a photograph.

In the confines of the book the photographer is faced with a choice of selecting only a proportion of the many available pictures. My aim has been to choose individual photographs that build up a picture of the county as each page is turned. Some views are familiar, many are new – small corners of Devon that have remained unchanged for centuries. Here too are the bustling towns and cities, the superb beaches and fishing ports, and of course the tourists' honeypots.

I would be pleased to feel that having looked through this book the reader is encouraged to explore for themselves some of the delights of Devon that otherwise they may never have visited.

PETER THOMAS
EXETER 1995

THE COAST

South Devon's coast is generally kinder than its northern shore. Bolberry Down lies between Salcombe and Hope Cove and on its gentler slopes the first foxgloves are beginning to appear.

Likened to dragon's teeth, treacherous rock formations are revealed by the receding
tide at Hartland Quay, North Devon.

The coast of South Devon has seen many a doomed ship lost on its shore.
Fortunately the crew survived the loss of this stricken vessel in 1992.

The Harbour wall in the North Devon village of
Clovelly has withstood the full might of the
Atlantic gales for centuries.

Winding down to the sea the famous
cobbled street at Clovelly brings the visitor
down to the harbour, here viewed through
an ancient archway.

The harbour at Teignmouth provides a quieter refuge than the foreshore.
It is still a place to see fishermen about their work. A passenger ferry crosses the
harbour to Shaldon.

Bright fishing floats create a carnival image in Kingswear harbour, South Devon.

Fishing nets, Brixham.
Inset: divers about to explore a wreck off Berry Head,
South Devon.

The limestone cliffs of Berry Head are a haven for seabirds and is the site of a
Napoleonic fort overlooking the Channel. The headland is a country park, attracting
thousands of visitors.

Newfoundland Bay from the clifftop at Froward Point. Just around the point, beyond
the pines, is the spectacular entrance to Dartmouth Harbour. Excellent coastal walks
follow the clifftop on National Trust land.

The view from Bolt Head to Salcombe. The Kingsbridge Estuary beyond is one of the finest in Devon, especially when seen from the gardens of 'Overbecks' in the National Trust property at Sharpitor House.

Sunset over the Exe estuary at Exmouth.

Lundy Island. Visitors queue for the *Oldenberg* which will ferry them back to the mainland. The first Marine Nature Reserve in the country, the waters surrounding Lundy contain many important marine species.

The Yealm Estuary winds through marvellous wooded countryside and, though close
to the city of Plymouth, it has escaped the hands of the developers. Upriver are the
idyllic villages of Noss Mayo and Newton Ferrers.

Boats ride the gentle tides on the estuary of the River Axe.
Inset: the bleached timbers of an ancient barge lie on the wide sandy flats where the
Taw and Torridge rivers run into the sea on the North Devon coast.

Sand dunes at Braunton Burrows form a barrier between the sea and North Devon's principal town, Barnstaple. The massive dune complex supports plantlife found nowhere else in the county, and in winter is the ideal place for quiet walks.

It was the mild winter climate that saw the town of Torquay rise to the height of its mid Victorian elegance and grandeur. Today as the English Riviera it remains the county's most popular resort.

Enthralled, children watch a Punch and Judy show, Torbay.

Sunset burnishes the sea at Sidmouth, Devon's most elegant resort.
Inset: little has changed since sailing ships tied up here, the quay at Dartmouth retains the
enduring charm of bygone days.

The bright blue sea and white buildings give this view of Appledore a Mediterranean feel.
This North Devon port has long been famed for shipbuilding.

The harbour, Lynmouth.

A replica of Sir Francis Drake's *Golden Hind* at Brixham.

Despite taking the full force of any sea gales, pine trees grow on the cliffs
overlooking the entrance to the Dart estuary, South Devon.

Inset: the Pilchard Inn, Burgh Island, off Bigbury-on-Sea.

Thirty houses in the South Devon village of Hallsands were swept away
during a violent storm in 1917. It is said that the dredging of millions of tons of
sand to help in the building of Plymouth Dock led to the sea's encroachment.

Gravestones at St Werburgh's church, Wembury in South Devon, have withstood
the gales of centuries.

The silhouette of Sir Francis Drake's statue on
Plymouth Hoe symbolises Devon's illustrious
maritime heritage.

King William's statue overlooks the gateway to the Royal William Yard, Stonehouse Plymouth. By far the most impressive group of buildings in the city, the dockyard has played a key role in Britain's maritime history.

Plymouth has had to come to terms with the reduction of naval forces in the city. The port remains an important shipbuilding and refitting yard and here the Royal Fleet Auxiliary *Brambleleaf* lies in the safe anchorage of the Hamoaze.

The impressive facade of The Royal Naval College, Dartmouth, overlooks the historic anchorage. Built at the turn of the century the Britannia college replaced ancient hulks of wooden warships which previously served as officer cadet training establishments.

Hope Cove, South Devon, nestles behind the cliffs of Bolt Tail, seen in the distance.

Sunset over the River Exe at Topsham

Winter sunshine bathes the red sandstone cliffs at Sidmouth.
Inset: Budleigh Salterton is renowned for its air of quiet gentility. The Victorian artist Millais
stayed here and his painting 'The Boyhood of Raleigh' is said to have been inspired by the place.

A visitor to Lundy discovers the dramatic coastline.

Hidden in a valley in the far north of the county, this beautiful waterfall cascades over
the cliff at Spekes Mill Mouth.

Dartmouth Castle and church (far bank) stand sentinel at the mouth of Dartmouth
Harbour. In times past a chain ran across to Kingswear Castle (near bank) and barred
the harbour entrance to unfriendly shipping.
Inset: upriver the village of Dittisham sits at the edge of the River Dart.

Solitude - Braunton Sands, North Devon.

TOWNS & VILLAGES

Otterton is one of the most visited villages in East Devon. The combination of farms
and cottages form a picturesque scene, completed by a stream running
through the village.

South Devon lays claim to any number of charming seaside villages.
One of the best known is at Hope Cove, consisting of Inner and Outer Hope.
At Inner Hope is The Square, a cluster of traditional thatched cottages.

Exeter is the capital city of Devon. Much of the attraction of the city is found away
from its centre, as here, at the head of the canal. Now home to a maritime museum, it
was once at the heart of the city's brisk shipping trade.

Ide village lies on the outskirts of Exeter. The stream in front of this pretty group of cottages, known as 'The College', is also a road!

South Pool on the Kingsbridge estuary.

Cottage and church nestling in the
Teign Valley at Ashton.

A thatcher completes a new ridge on a cottage
next to Dittisham church.

'Old Maid's' Cottage
at Lee near Ilfracombe.

Roadside surprises are not uncommon in Devon.
Huge millstones flank the door of an old mill near
Crediton mid Devon.

Branscombe, East Devon.
Note the repaired thatch.

Brand new thatch adds a golden glow to this cottage
at Lustleigh.

A group of cottages at Buckland in the Moor, southern Dartmoor.

A superb example of the stone mason's art. The granite frontage of a group of alms houses in Moretonhampstead on Dartmoor, dating from 1637.

A facade of another kind at South Molton incorporates a
number of architectural styles. The building dates from early
nineteenth century

An evocation of the gentility of rural Devon in times past.
Antique trunk and cases at Staverton railway station,
now a private line.

The floral splendours of the Rougemont Gardens in Exeter offer a peaceful haven in
the heart of the city. The medieval Athelstan's tower
rises in the distance.

The solid grandeur of Exeter Cathedral and the Bishop's Palace stand in the
heart of the city.

The breathtaking vaulted roof, Exeter Cathedral.
Inset: Exeter's Cathedral Close retains a number of architectural treasures including
this studded oak door.

A leaded window in Tuckers Hall, Exeter. The Hall is the home of the City's oldest
Guild and is one of the country's finest medieval buildings. Its atmosphere is unique.

A view of Exeter above Trew's Weir.
In former times ships sailed up to the city beyond the weir.

Topsham was once amongst the most important ports in England,
handling much of the woollen export trade for the county.

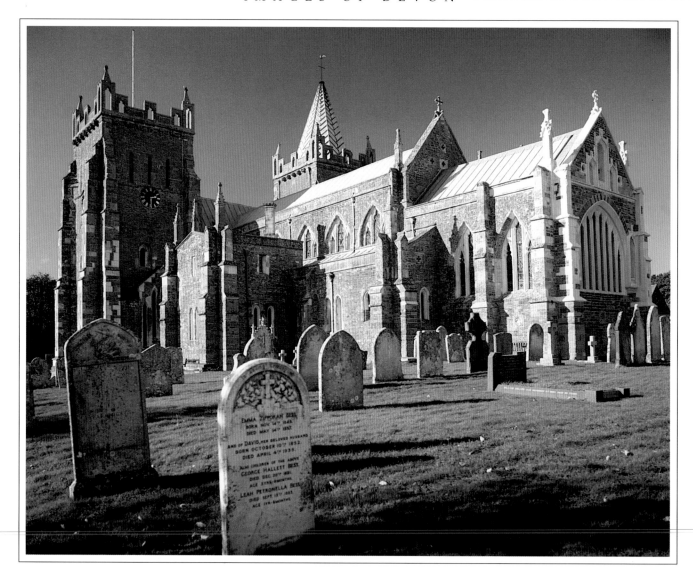

St Mary's church at Ottery St Mary, established in 1337.
The similarity to Exeter Cathedral in building style is marked. Both were built under
the direction of Bishop Grandison

Queen Anne's Walk in Barnstaple was originally built as an Exchange and dates from
the early eighteenth century. The colonnade houses the 'Tome Stone', an ancient stone
on which merchants sealed their bargains. Queen Anne's statue overlooks the square.

Totnes.

The ancient Guildhall at Totnes dates from the mid sixteenth century, although the
open loggia was added in 1897. It houses the Court room (inset), beautifully panelled,
with a coat of arms in plaster above the mayoral chair.

Between tree-lined banks the River Torridge runs towards Taddiport Bridge at
Great Torrington.

Built in 1869-75 for Sir John Heathcoat-Amory, grandly
overlooking his textile mill at Tiverton, Knightshayes
is now in the care of the National Trust.
The gardens here are particularly fine.

Home of the Earls of Devon, Powderham Castle has been
in the Courtenay family for six hundred years. A fortified
manor house, surrounded by a deer park, the castle
commands superb views over the Exe estuary.

The superb seventeenth century gatehouse
at Bradstone Manor, near Tavistock.

Once the home of the Victorian cleric and writer the Rev.
Sabine Baring Gould (author of *Onward Christian Soldiers*),
Lew Trenchard Manor, now an hotel, has been described
as an interesting confection of building styles.

Haldon Belvedere situated high on the Haldon ridge is the
most prominent landmark in the Exeter area.
It was built in 1788 by Sir Robert Palk to commemorate
General Stringer Lawrence, his friend and benefactor.

The popularity of converting barns into dwellings has seen a decline in
traditional agricultural buildings in their original state. Barns, such as this one near
Chagford, though in sad repair, are an essential part of the landscape.

The beautiful simplicity of a remote country church:
St Mary's in the evocatively named village of Honeychurch, near Sampford Courtenay.
Inset left: intricate carving on the rood screen at St James' church Swimbridge.
Inset right: the painted screen at Holy Trinity, Gidleigh.

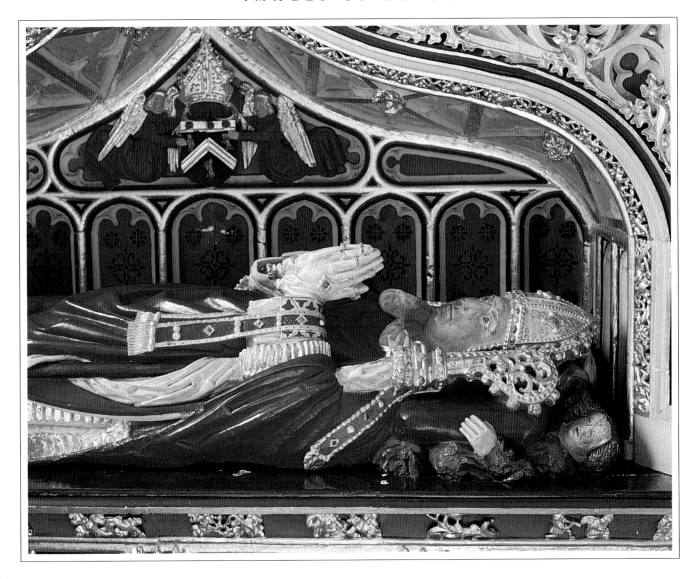

The effigy of Bishop Hugh Oldham (d.1519), at Exeter Cathedral.

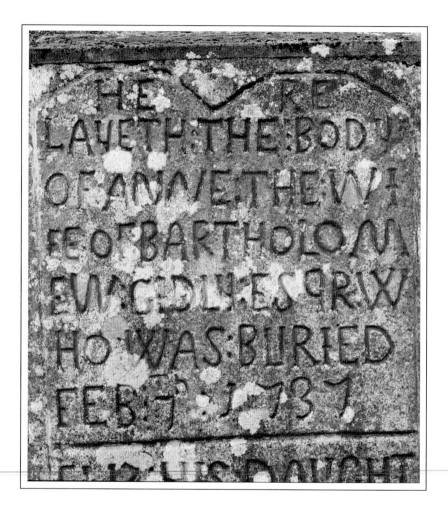

A simple tombstone in Gidleigh churchyard.

The church of St Michael de Rupe, Brentor, has the most extraordinary site of any church
in Devon, and sweeping views of Dartmoor can be seen from its lofty granite pinnacle.

An elaborate horse trough stands in
Great Torrington's wide and pleasant street,
the handsome red brick Town Hall behind.

A flower-bedecked street in Budleigh Salterton.

Two views of tourism: sea trips at Torquay.
Inset: gleaming brass at Cockington Forge.

Harbourside lights, Torquay, create a dazzling backdrop to the nightlife of the resort.

A view across Plymouth Hoe into the heart of the city.

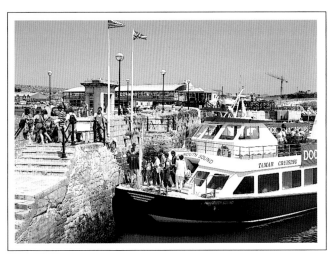

The Mayflower Steps from where the Pilgrim Fathers embarked at Sutton Harbour, Plymouth. These days boat trips are taken to the nearby Royal Navy yard.

Fishing boats tied up in Sutton Pool, Plymouth, the elegant Customs House beyond.

Isambard Kingdom Brunel's famous railway bridge spans the River Tamar, Linking Devon with Cornwall.

Dawlish, where mainline tracks run close to the lapping waves; one of Britain's most thrilling train journeys.

RURAL DEVON

Bluebells carpet a woodland glade near Honiton.

Rusty rollers lie in the lush grassland near Brampford Speke
a few miles from Exeter.

Top left:
A fifteenth century bridge spans the River Torridge
at Bideford.

Top right:
Mirrored in the still waters, a bridge spans the Grand
Western Canal. Once a major transport link, horse-drawn
barges now carry tourists through the tranquil countryside
near Tiverton.

Left:
One of Devon's loveliest bridges crosses the
River Dart at Staverton.

On the border between Devon and Cornwall near
Sydenham Damerel stands the ancient Horse Bridge.

Pleasure cruisers patiently wait their turn to enter the
pound lock on the Exeter canal near the Double Locks Hotel.

Sunset over the Taw Estuary,
near Barnstaple.

The sweeping arches of the Calstock viaduct take the
River Tamar elegantly in their stride.

Winter mists rise from the silent River Culm in the Exe Valley, near Rewe.

Popular with visitors, and little wonder, for the scene at Bickleigh is one to be treasured.

Sunrise gilds the morning sky over the Exe.

Scene from a bygone age. An ancient vessel tied up at Morwellham Quay,
now a living industrial museum.

Rich farmland in the Exe Valley near Thorverton.

Summer, and harvesting begins at Upton Pyne near Exeter.

Grazing cattle near Cadbury.
Inset: harvesting near Copplestone.

Wild poppy flowers paint the landscape at Caton near Ashburton.

Harvest home at Brampford Speke.

Passing scenes of country life:
a disused corn spreader, Yeoford near Crediton (top left);
driving sheep on a Dartmoor lane (top right); ploughing on an ancient meadowland
(lower left); an outbuilding blossoms near Broadclyst (lower right).

Wild flowers border a field of ripening corn.
Shobrooke, near Crediton.

The industrial museum at Morwellham Quay recreates the
atmosphere of Victorian life in Devon.

Scenes at a steam fair near Exeter.

A lane near Dunkeswell.

The ancient mill at Oakford Bridge near the Somerset and Exmoor border.
The gradual disappearance of such buildings, along with the old farmsteads,
has led to a rapid decline in the Barn Owl population in Devon (inset).

Devon has a richness in wild plant life, almost beyond compare. Its varied habitats
provide fertile support in which common, and many rare species abound. Wild garlic
in full bloom (main picture) near Tiverton; Stonecrop flowers on a sunny wall at
Wembury Point (inset left); frosted spikes of Cow Parsley on the River Culm.

• CIDER MAKING •

Apple tree prosper, bud bloom and bear,
That we may have plenty of cider next year,
And where there's a barrel we hope there are ten,
That we may have cider when we come again.

Cider making has been part of Devon's farming
scene since the time of the Norman Conquest
and though orchards have been in decline, new
interests in the traditions of the craft have seen
a revival in recent years.

Cider apples are harvested in the late Autumn
and are chopped to form a pulp rich in juices.
The pulp is spread in a stone trough beneath
the cider press, alternating with layers of straw.
Finally the press is lowered on to the pulp and
straw, squeezing out the golden liquid. Here
the newly pressed cider is sampled as it flows
from the trough beneath the press.

Stored in wooden barrels to complete
fermentation, the cider is ready to be drunk
within weeks. Devon cider ranges from sweet
to eye-watering dry.

The photographs show Mr Brimblecombe
making cider on his farm at Dunsford.

Autumn colours show in the sunlit woodland at Cove,
near Bampton.

Golden leaves strewn in a sunken lane near Bampton are typical
of an autumnal Devon scene.

Woodbury Common east of Exeter provides an important heathland habitat for many plant and animal species. At its highest point, hidden among majestic beech trees, is a prehistoric hill fort with sweeping ramparts.

Mysterious Wistman's Wood, Dartmoor. Here amid broken granite boulders, twisted dwarf oaks, festooned with ferns and lichen, struggle to survive in an inhospitable moorland landscape.

• COUNTRY CRAFTS •

In times past the countryman relied on skills such as hurdle-making
(main picture and top) to provide a living. A revival in interest has given a new lease
of life to many such crafts. A skilled wood worker completes a wheelbarrow made
entirely of wood (above).

A vast concrete dam spans a deep-cut valley on the edge of Dartmoor
at Burrator Reservoir. Dense woodland and high moors are home of the Buzzard,
Devon's largest bird of prey.

Fields of wild flowers a thing of the past? Not in Exeter's Valley Parks where there is a
policy to recreate meadows as they used to be. Here a host of buttercups wave
beneath a blue summer sky. Inset: Pyramidal Orchid.

Near Hollocombe Hamlets, Crediton.
Famous red Devon soil contrasts with the field of golden oil-seed rape.
Inset: cowslip.

Red Deer have migrated into many parts of Devon from nearby Exmoor.
A stag jealously guards his hinds against possible rivals (inset left),
and a hind is poised ready for flight (inset right). Rowan berries contrast
with a blue autumn sky (backgound).

Unloved by farmers, the fox remains one of Devon's most populous wild creatures.
Its handsome looks and smart reputation endear it to those who have nothing to
loose by its predatory habits.

High above the Teign Valley lie Tottiford, Kennick and Trenchford reservoirs, built in
the past century to supply water to the growing population of Torbay. Bordered by
Rhododendrons the lakes are an important recreational and leisure facility for walkers
and fishermen.

Springtime in Lydford Gorge. Now owned by the National Trust,
the River Lyd and its beautiful valley provide superb walking country on
Dartmoor's western edge.

Haldon Forest, near Exeter. The stark majesty of a beech tree in winter contrasts
vividly with the cascading greenery of beech woods in early summer.

The glorious beech avenue at Gittisham.

Shafts of autumn sunlight at East Hill Strips near Ottery St Mary.

Carpeting the woodland floor, pungent-scented wood garlic
flowers in the early summer.

A woodland walk near Christow.

LIVING
IN DEVON

Fairs of all kinds highlight the summer months in Devon. The Devon County Show held at Westpoint near Exeter in May each year is the premier agricultural and trade fair and attracts well over 100 000 people over three days. In contrast each village has its own summer fair. Lustleigh show is held in the early summer. Here morris dancers perform against the backdrop of Dartmoor's hills.

Sidmouth Folk Festival is one of the largest of its kind in Europe, attracting performers from throughout the world.

The English Civil War raged throughout Devon for many years.
Here, in more peaceful times, members of the Sealed Knot re-enact a battle in the
grounds of Powderham Castle.

Contrasting venues to attract the summer tourists.
Above: water shutes and leisure pools at Goodrington near Torquay.
Below: Victorian ladies and gentlemen reflect a more genteel age at
Morwellham's 'living' museum.

All the fun of the fair at Goodrington where a
Helter Skelter provides traditional fairground
entertainment.

Also intended to put heart in mouth, absailing
at Haytor on Dartmoor, one of the new leisure
pursuits offered by adventure holidays.

But some prefer a good old-fashioned snooze in the sun.
Deck chairs on the seafront at Paignton.

'She sells seashells...'
Dawlish.

DARTMOOR
HEART OF
DEVON

Dartmoor National Park comprises 365 square miles of moorland and upland
farmland in the heart of the county of Devon. Famed for its mists, its Prison, and its
wild ponies, it is in fact one of Britain's most beautiful wild regions, as this view across
to Merrivale Quarry shows.

Haytor quarry. From here granite was shipped to London where it was used in the
construction of many of the capital's finest buildings.

• DARTMOOR GRANITE •

Dartmoor is a granite landscape, its older buildings seemingly as solid and strong as the valleys and tors around them. The fine church house of South Tawton, with lychgate and church beyond, all of granite (top left).

Old and new bridges span the East Dart river at Postbridge. The famous clapper bridge (foreground) stands on four granite piers surmounted by huge slabs weighing up to eight tons (left).

An old ash house near Lustleigh. Ashes from the kitchen fire would be stored here, later to be spread on the fields to reduce acidity in the moorland soil.

Becky Falls, near Manaton, famed tourist 'honeypot', but perhaps best seen in winter
when the Becka Brook in full spate cascades over the giant boulders.

Spinster's Rock near Drewsteignton:
the remains of a prehistoric burial mound.

Granite cross on Week Down near Chagford. Many such
crosses provided waymarks across the featureless moor for
early travellers to follow. Most date from medieval times.

Dartmoor contains more visible prehistoric remains than any other
landscape in the world. Scorhill stone circle is one such enigmatic site.
Inset: Drizzlecombe Menhir stands sentinel at the head of a remote Dartmoor valley.
It is associated with Bronze Age stone rows, cairns and other monuments in the area.

Bowerman's Nose near Manaton on Dartmoor's eastern flank. This natural column of rock is associated with a number of local legends.

Dartmoor ponies are famed the world over. Hardy and spirited, they can weather the harshest winters on a meagre diet of moorland grass, heather and even gorse!

Summer clouds billow high over Sheepstor.

A place for quiet meditation: the West Dart river above Hexworthy Bridge.

Winter frosts turn the ground to iron and the high moorland landscape
becomes a bleak and inhospitable place. Frost encases bracken (inset).

Like fallen soldiers: this line of beeches was decimated
by a winter gale.

Rust-coloured bracken and heather clad the high moorland
valley slopes in winter.

Lee Moor clayworks on the south-western edge of Dartmoor reveal the impact of man's hand on a fragile landscape.